10 easy ways to earn money online from instamojo

Deepak Yadav

ISBN 978-93-5667-035-8
© Deepak Yadav 2022
Published in India 2022 by Pencil

A brand of
One Point Six Technologies Pvt. Ltd.
123, Building J2, Shram Seva Premises,
Wadala Truck Terminal, Wadala (E)
Mumbai 400037, Maharashtra, INDIA
E connect@thepencilapp.com
W www.thepencilapp.com

Author biography

I am an infopreneur and i make money online.

I have seen many ups and downs in my life.

But the year 2016 was the worst time of my life because at this time I was very much troubled by depression and anxiety.

I made every effort to get out of this mental state.

Today I am far away from depression and anxiety.

In fact my life changed after the depression.

I learned many life lessons during this time and I want to teach this lesson to you through my books.

I hope you get to learn a lot from my books which might change your career and life.

CONTENTS

Introduction

Nowadays you will find many online ways to earn money, about which you will have good knowledge, but there are many such ways about which very few people know and today we will tell you about one of those ways by which you can make money online sitting at home. can earn.

In this growing world of technology, earning money has become as easy as it is difficult because we do not have a good knowledge about the ways in which money can be earned.

Many times we do this that we read about some methods on the internet and without taking deep knowledge we start working on it which does not give us good results so it is important that you go to any field then related to it. You have all the information.

Today we are going to tell you about such a platform, about which you have hardly heard and if you have heard, then you may not be fully aware about it.

So stay with this article till the end so that you can get all the information related to this topic.

The name of the platform we are talking about today is Instamojo.

Have you heard about it?

If not then today you will get complete information about it, so let's start and first of all know what is Instamojo?

Instamojo is a very popular free payment gateway in India, about which very few people know.

This is a platform in which India makes its indigenous online payment and due to lack of knowledge about it, crores of people use foreign online payment platform, which gives very little benefit to India.

Although it is not that no one uses it, this platform is very famous among those who know about it.

It is used by many big digital marketers and freelancers etc. Not only this, but many people also earn money by using it.

If we talk about the users who use them, then they believe that this is a great platform and it is also very easy to use.

Under this, the facility of online selling and online payment is provided to small business people.

This is such a good platform that not only online payment but also online store can be created in which you can also sell your product, about which you will know in further detail.

If we talk about their features, then under this you get such features which are very easy to use and you get them for free.

When you use it to upload and sell your product, you can get your payment from this platform.

Also, here you also get the option of delivery, in this you will get s.m.s. There is also a facility to do this as well as Google Analytics integration can also be done inside it.

So this was some things related to Instamojo.

Now we tell you how you can create your account inside it.

How to create account on Instamojo?

If you want to learn how to create an account on Instamojo, then read the steps given below carefully and follow them.

Here you will get all the details and you will not face any problem in creating an account.

Step-1: To create an account on Instamojo, first you have to go to the Instamojo official website and open it.

You can directly Instamojo. You can login by going to com, after which you will get the option of sign up in the right corner.

Step-2: When you click on this sign up option, after that you will get two options first option Merchant and second buyer.

Now because here you are being told about how to earn money online, so you have to click on Merchant.

Step-3: After this a page will open in front of you, in which you will get many types of options so that you will be able to login such as Google Account, Facebook and Email ID.

You will need to enter an email address and a password.

Step-4: After this you will be asked to enter the mobile number, after which another OTP will come on your phone number through which you will have to verify and after that you can sign up.

Step-5: When you do the verification from the mobile phone, then you will come across two options of free online store and payment, in this you have to click on the payment option where you will set your username.

Step-6: You will get an option to set a username, in which you can select any username of your choice which is available, which you will know by check availability.

Step-7: You will see on your screen that a question is being asked to you that What type of business are you? And together two options will appear of Individual and Register Organization.

If you are creating a personal account then you will click on the individual option where you will be asked Are you a proprietor? Below which there will be an option of Yes and No, you have to select that and proceed.

Step-8: After this you will have to answer some business-related questions, after which you will be asked to enter PAN card number, name and address.

Step-9: After this you have to fill your bank details in which you have to enter account number, IFSC code and account holder name.

Step-10: When you have done all these things, your Instamojo account will be setup and you will be entered in your dashboard.

You do not incur any charges for setting up an account and here we give you some information about the charges you will incur-

If you use Credit & Debit Card, Net Banking or UPI service on your account then you will have to pay 2% per sale.

If you want, you can also submit KYC on this platform, its very easy in steps.

All you have to do is click on the submit KYC option on your dashboard and enter your product or service details.

Under this, you have to tell about the name of the product and its price, which can also be changed later.

After this, you have to upload the photo of its front side by entering your PAN card details, after that you have to enter some details of the bank.

Then you will be asked the address, state and pin code etc. After this you have to click on the option of submit for review and your KYC will be submitted.

As we told you that you can also create an online store on this platform which looks very attractive and looks exactly like a professional online store.

Here you can sell not only digital but also other content.

Now we tell you what are the steps to make online door here-

Step-1: After creating your account on this platform, you have to go to your dashboard where you will get the option of Create Online Thief on the left corner.

Step-2: Here you will be asked what name you want to name your store you can name your store as per your wish and you have to click on Next button where you have to enter social media link on online store.

In this you can put any link like Facebook, YouTube or Instagram profile link.

Although it is not necessary to complete it, if you do not want to enter any link, then you can click on the next option.

Step-3: Now you have to click on the options which you want to sell on your online store.

Here you will see many options such as physical product, digital product, service, event ticket and many more.

You can select any option and if you want, you can also select all these options.

Step-4: After this you have to select the category related to your business, now you click on the next option after which you will get the option to customize your store and after clicking on it you have to click on the next option again

Step-5: Here you have to create a link for your online store, which is very important, with this link people will be able to access your store, so it is important that your link is unique.

After doing this, you will get the option of Create Store, after clicking on which your online store will be ready.

Step-6: After this the final step is that you have to click on your Verify My Mobile Store button.

In this way you know how you can create and take advantage of all the accounts on Instamojo.

Now we will tell you further how money can be earned from this platform.

You will find many ways to earn money on this platform, out of which today we are going to tell you the top 10 easy ways which are very popular and easy too.

On this platform, you can easily earn a lot of money by selling any of your products or services online.

So let's know which are the ways which are very popular on Instamojo-

1. By Selling Physical Products

There will be many people who do not know that digital products as well as physical products can be sold on Instamojo and earn money.

Today we are going to tell you about this method, how you can earn money by selling physical products on it.

The first way to earn money from Instamojo is by selling physical products, which is very easy, just for this you have to add your product to Instamojo.

Step-1: First of all we will talk about how to add physical product on your account, then for that you have to follow the given steps-

Step-2: First you have to go to the dashboard on your Instamojo account.

Step-3: You can see on the screen that in the left side you will see an option of add product on which you have to click.

Step-4: After this the option of product category will appear in front of you, you will click on it, under which you will see an option of physical product.

Step-5: When you will select the option of physical product, then you will have to enter many types of information such as-

Details: The first option will come in front of you, in which you will get the title of the product, description in which you will tell something about your product, price, if there is any discount on it, then you will tell about it, quantity in which you will tell about the quantity of your product. I will tell you the order limit quantity i.e. the quantity one can order the product and the maximum shipping day in which you will tell in how many days the customers will get their order.

Along with this, you will have to upload some photos of your product, you will have to fill all these details in this option.

Variants: The next option comes of Variant, in which you have to tell how your product is, that is, if your product is available in different colors or sizes, then you have to enter its details.

It may be that the Variant option is disabled on your screen, in such a situation you have to enable it first, after that you can write the details of the product.

Categories: After this you get the option of category in which you can create any category according to you.

But you have to choose the category related to your product, as if you have a product that comes under food,

then you have to choose a category related to food.

Reselling: This is such an option that if you enable it, your product can be promoted by someone else, in return for which you will have to pay some commission to it.

If you do not want to do this then you leave it disabled and if you enable this feature then your product is more likely to sell.

It completely depends on you whether you want to give your product in the hands of any other person or not because on every sale you have to pay him some commission so you can use this option according to your need.

SEO setting: There will be many of you people who would like your online store to rank in Google and more and more people know about it so that people can visit your online shop and increase traffic.

For this, you get an option of such an aceo setting in which you can optimize SEO.

Under this, you can apply various types of meta tags, descriptions and tags related to your product or service and can do other SEO related work.

It has the advantage that your store reaches more and more people, that is, whenever someone searches on Google for the tag that you have entered, then your store will also be visible to them.

You can simply understand that this is an easy way to get your online store ranked on Google.

Advanced: Here you will get some advanced features from where you can do some extra settings for your account like if a customer buys any product from your store then you can show him thank you note etc.

Under this, you can also set the URL where the customer after making the payment will reach a new page whose URL you have given, this is mostly done to bring the new product in front of them.

Apart from this, when a customer visits your store, you can show them a welcome note, you can do many such tasks inside it.

In this way, to sell a physical product, you get so many features that define your product well.

This is also important because these things attract customers to you.

Now it comes to how products are sold here and how do you get money?

The answer is that whenever you add a product to your online store, here you get a product link.

You can share this link with your friends, relatives or people around you so that maximum traffic can come to your store.

Your link appears as a product card on your online store and when someone clicks on this link, they can reach your online store and place their orders and you get the payment instantly.

The way of selling physical products is very easy, you will not have any problem in this, you just have to try that the link of your store reaches as many people as possible so that you can take advantage.

On Instamojo, along with the convenience of having your product delivered to you, you also get the feature that you can also levy shipping charges on your product.

Even you can keep your shipping charges higher than the price of the product which you can decide according to your profit.

You can do this in two ways, the first way is- if you want, you can fix flat shipping charge for all the orders, even if the customer buys one or more products, that means, the payment will be taken as shipping for only one product. .

Another way is to fix separate shipping charges for each product which is the latest update of Instamojo.

When you create the link for the product, then at that time you will get the option to add shipping charges and you can easily reach the product to the customer.

2. By Selling E-Books

The most trending in the world of freelancing is e-book.

You must have known about E-book , you must have read about it in many websites and seen in the videos what it is after all.

Do you know what an e-book is?

If not, then let us give you some information about it.

E-book means electronic book which you can read on your mobile or laptop anytime and anywhere.

Nowadays its demand has become very high because it can also be read offline and today in the world of internet, you will get ebook on every topic.

If you also have the skill that you can prepare and sell a good book through the Internet, then you can earn a lot of money by uploading it on Instamojo.

After creating an e-book, the biggest problem is where we have to sell it because you will find many platforms where you can sell e-books.

But it is very difficult to choose a platform in which you get all the features easily and it is easy to take payment.

But you will be surprised to know that e-book can also be sold on our India's payment gateway platform Instamojo, inside which you can easily get payment by using the payment link.

Instamojo is a platform where you can sell physical products as well as digital products and you will get many options inside it, one of them is e-book.

If you have prepared your e-book and you are looking for a platform to sell it, which can make your e-book popular among more and more people and you will not face any problem in taking its payment. Instamojo can prove to be a best platform if you do not have to face it.

If you have not prepared the e-book and you do not understand which topic you should choose for it, then there is nothing to worry about it.

On whichever topic you have good knowledge, you can make it your title, under this you can prepare a book related to travel, related to child development or even about new ways of income.

Before selling your book here, you need to know about adding a digital product to your online store because as you know that e-book is a digital product so without adding it you cannot upload it.

So let's know how to add digital product to your online store-

The way we add a physical product, in the same way a digital product is also added, the only difference is that in the digital product, when we fill the details of our e-book such as title, discription and any other details, then it is added as an add. While doing this, we have to upload a digital file.

As we are talking about e-book here i.e. you will upload the digital file of your e-book and as you know these files can be downloaded and the best thing here is that max 2GB Can upload any single digital file.

When you prepare your e-book and process it further to sell on this platform, you will see that the book can be published in such an easy way that you will be surprised.

Here everything related to SEO is taken care of, so that there is no possibility of any kind of mistake and one of its features is that you can go and edit its description or price at any time.

Now we tell you how to sell e-book on Instamojo?

To sell e-book on Instamojo, first you have to create your account, which we have told you above and add your digital products.

When you will fill all the details related to your e-book in it, then you will get the upload option, on which you have to click and upload your e-book.

Here you also get this feature that you can promote your e-book by sharing it on many types of social media platforms such as Facebook, Instagram and WhatsApp.

The best thing here is that whenever someone buys your book by clicking on your link, you get his money within 2 days.

Uploading an e-book is the easiest and best way to earn money because whenever someone clicks on your link and buys your e-book, then you get money.

If you want to know how you can get your payout, then for this you will have to create a payment link.

To generate the payment link, you have to go to the dashboard of your profile where you will get the option of payment link.

Here you will be asked some details, after which your link will be prepared through which you can collect your payment.

You will get all kinds of facilities here, which will make working even easier.

From adding digital products to uploading and receiving payments, all the work can be done in Instamojo, hence it is called the best payment gateway.

3. By Selling Video Courses

Do you want to earn money by selling any video courses online?

If yes, then today we are going to tell you an easy way to earn money by selling video courses on Instamojo.

First of all, you have to know that what is a video course after all?

The meaning of a video course is to record your skill in a video and sell it on an online platform so that people can learn something from it.

In today's technology world, most of the people use videos etc. in online platforms to learn any new thing.

Whether it is to learn to make small things such as hand craft or to get information related to any other field, everyone resorts to video courses.

Nowadays, studies have also started with the help of online video courses, so if you have a video course that you want to earn money by selling, then you can earn a lot by using Instamojo.

Today, when you look around you, you will find many such people who are earning a lot of money by selling video courses on their website and there are many people who can prepare video courses but they do not have any such platform. where he can easily get paid by selling his video courses.

In such a situation, we recommend you to sell video courses on Instamojo because it is a very reliable platform and the payment amount can also be easily obtained here.

So let us now tell you how the video course can be sold on Instamojo and how to get money-

Here also you have to follow the same process that you saw in the above 2 methods i.e. by creating your account on Instamojo, you have to add products but here you have to add digital product because video course comes under digital product.

Let us know step by step how to sell the video course-

Step-1: When you go to the dashboard of your profile, there you will get an option of digital file.

Step-2: By clicking on it you will see that you will get an option of upload, after clicking on which you will upload your video course.

Step-3: Below this you will see an option of Add Image, which you can put any image of your video course.

Step-4: After doing this, you have to select the title of your video course, here you have to put the title of the video course related to the subject you have prepared.

Step-5: Below that you will get the description box where you have to write some things related to your video course which can define your video course well.

You can also attach a link to your video course in your description box, which will make it much easier for the customer to know about your video course.

Step-6: After this, you have to select the price of your video course, you can fix the price as much as you want to sell your video course.

Here you also get the option of pay you want, in which if you have kept the price of any of your video courses at Rs 50, then you will get Rs 50 as well as if a customer wants, you can also pay extra.

Therefore Instamojo proves to be a good platform to sell videos.

Step-7: Next option you will get limit number of downloads on buyer it means how many times a customer can download your video course, here you can decide all these things.

Step-8: After this you have to tell the quantity of your video course whether it is unlimited or minimum number of times it can be downloaded.

Step-9: After this you will get the category option in which you can choose any category related to the video call.

It is optional so you can leave it if you want.

Step-10: As we told you that here you also get the option of reselling, after enabling that someone else can also sell your video course so that on every sale you will have to pay him some commission.

The advantage of this is that the chances of selling your video course increase.

Step-11: If you want to rank the video course, then you also get the option of SEO where you can put a tag related to the video course so that whenever someone searches for that tag, your video course will be visible to them first.

Step-12: Here also you get the option of Advance in which options like Thank You Note, Redirect URL and Web Hook URL etc. are available.

After filling all the details in this way, your video course is ready to be sold.

If you want to see further how your video course is showing, then you can go to My Online Store on your dashboard to see that your video course is showing on the screen with all the details.

If you want, you can also do editing in it, in which you will get the option of Buy Now.

Here you will also get the option to share, through which you can reach your video course to as many people as possible.

You can copy your link here and share it with your friends, relatives or others on various platforms.

All the people who will click on this link of yours, there will definitely be some people who will buy your video course.

This platform is absolutely free and also reliable, so you get a lot of profit in selling such digital products.

Just as you know the process of receiving payment in e-book, here also the same process is applicable, you can get your payment through payment link.

4. By Selling Software

Who does not know about software in today's digital age?

You know that whatever work computer or mobile can do, it does not do it by itself, for this it needs commands and these commands are put in a category called computer or mobile which is called software.

Simply put, it is a program by which our computer or mobile works.

Developing or preparing software is a very important task which is a bit difficult to do but in today's era you will find many such apps, which has made this complicated task very easy.

It has become so easy that you can create a software in just a few minutes.

You must have known that it is very important to learn coding to prepare software and you should also have knowledge about the language related to it, but you will find such tools where you can prepare software without coding and without any language. And you can earn a lot of money by selling it.

Here we are going to tell you what is the best platform to sell software, but before that know how to make software?

You will find many applications for making software and you will also see many such websites from where you can learn about the tools to make software.

There are many websites where you can make software professionally and can also do customization, for this you may have to purchase a premium plan.

You can login to any application of your choice where you have to create your account with the help of email id and password.

Inside many applications, you will also get the guideline, by following which you will be able to make software, although there will be some applications that will take some charges to make software, but there are many applications which are absolutely free and you have the option of apps for free. will be found under it.

Now it comes to where and how to sell this software to reach more and more people so that you can earn extra money?

Most of the people use playstore to sell their software but when you publish any software or application on play store then you have to register on google play developer console and for this you have to pay 25$ as charge. But there are many people who do not have that much budget and they look for some such applications in which software can be sold for free and one such application is Instamojo.

Where you can sell your software absolutely free of cost and today we will tell you about selling software on Instamojo because you have read how reliable it is a platform from where you can get instant payment.

The method of selling software on Instamojo is very simple and the process is exactly the same as you read in video courses and e-books on how to earn money.

Here also you have to upload the software by going to the digital file and enter its image and other details, after which your software will be shown in your online store.

You can also share its link and promote it to reach more and more people.

If you do not want to make software, then you can hire a software developer to make your own software, although in this you will have to pay something to that software developer, so if you have a good budget then you can also adopt this method.

Apart from this, one way is to buy software from any platform and sell it on your online store.

For example, suppose you have bought a software from a platform for 10 thousand rupees and you want to earn money by selling it, then you can add it to your online store and fix its price accordingly.

For example, if you keep its price of Rs 1 thousand and if 10 people also buy this software, then you will get back what you paid and after that all the people who buy your software will be your earning.

In this way you can also earn money from Instamojo by selling software. On Instamojo you can get payment for your software in one click through payment link.

The possibility of earning more and more money from software is because nowadays every computer or mobile needs new software and without them mobile and computer cannot work.

So if you can create a software that can attract people towards you, then you can benefit greatly.

Apart from this, as you know that in some applications you do not need to learn coding, although it is also true that coding software is more secure, so what to say if you know coding.

If you also want to earn a lot of money by selling software and want to take advantage of good and best features of Instamojo, then download this application and create account and create your online store, you can easily sell digital products like software here. Huh.

There are many other ways given by which you can earn money by working on Instamojo, so stay connected with us till the end.

5. By Selling Graphic Design

Today's era is the digital age and all the work has started happening online.

In this digital age, you must have seen many websites on your internet, on which you will get a lot of different types of information.

To make these websites, there are some things which are very important and work to attract people, one of them is graphic design, whose demand has increased a lot today.

People do not have enough time that they can do graphic design for their website themselves and there are many people who do not have knowledge of them, in such a situation, they are looking for people who can do graphic design for their website. Can prepare

If you are wondering what is Graphic Design, then let us tell you that it is a skill in which you give an attractive look to any text through word, image and color, such as you must have created posters and posters in your surrounding area. You must have seen banners, which promote different companies.

The graphic designer makes these posters and banners.

You will find many people on the Internet who can buy graphic designs from you to promote their company or website.

So if you want to make your career on this then it can prove to be a great way.

Where we are going to tell you how you can make and sell your graphic design.

Although you will find many platforms on social media from where you can provide graphic design to people, but Instamojo is a platform where you can add your graphic design in online store and make it available in front of people round the clock.

Graphic design is also added to the digital file in the same way as you know about adding e-books, video courses and software.

The advantage of adding graphic design to instamojo is that whenever visitors visit your online store, they will easily see your graphic design and they can buy the design they like because here it is related to graphic design. All the information like its price, description, images etc. will already be uploaded by you.

If you have created a creative graphic design then there will definitely be some visitors who will buy that design.

If you are wondering where to make graphic design, then there are many software on social media from where it is very easy to create graphic design such as Canva, Photoshop, Crello etc.

You do not need to do any course to do graphic design, it depends on your creativity and skills.

However, if you want, you will also get courses related to it.

On Instamojo, you can edit the details of your graphic design at any time and promote your graphic design by sharing its link on many platforms.

If you want, through various social media platforms, you can find out which topic related graphic design is more in demand nowadays and you can add it to Instamojo by creating related graphic design from that.

In this way, you also get a chance to earn money by selling graphic designs on Instamojo and can get paid using the payment link.

6. By Selling Event Tickets

Are you an event organizer and looking for a platform to sell your event tickets where you can easily find a customer?

So Instamojo gives you this opportunity that you can easily find customers here and reduce the burden of selling your tickets a little because here you get customers easily.

The third option you get on Instamojo after physical and digital products is event tickets where you can also earn money by selling event tickets online.

The way to sell tickets for any type of event becomes very easy on this platform because here you get all the features through which you can also sell your event tickets at different prices, about which you will get details. The information is given below.

Here you can also sell VIP Pass and Normal Pass separately and the best part is that using Instamojo's best features, booking event tickets becomes much easier.

Here we are going to tell you what options you get under event tickets and how you can organize the event yourself and sell its tickets.

Let us first know how the event ticket link is created?

For this follow the steps given below-

Step-1 : First you have to go to the dashboard of your Instamojo account and click on the option of add product where you will see the option of event ticket after digital product and physical product.

Step-2: After this you will see some options, out of which the first option will be add image in which you will upload the image of the event ticket.

Step-3: After this you have to tell what is the discounted price of the event you are organizing.

Step-4 : After doing this you will tell about the price of the event ticket and its number such as the maximum number of tickets that a customer can buy at a time and the minimum number of tickets he will have to buy.

Step-5: After this you will see an option for the type of event, under which you will get two types of options that are virtual event and in person event.

Let us tell you about these two events in a little detail-

Virtual Event: This option is selected when you organize a virtual event or an online event.

In online events, your guests (customers) connect with you through online platforms such as Google Meet, Zoom or any other platform.

When you select this option, then you will have to provide some details under it such as you will have to give a link to the platform through which your guests will join you in the event and also you can set a password if you want.

Apart from this, you will have to tell the time of start and end of the event along with the date.

Here you get an option of check box under which you can send email to your guest as reminder 1 hour before the start of event and also send payment receipt details so this platform is very popular for organizing event Is

In-Person Event: By the name of in-person event you can understand what it is.

Under In-Person Events, your guests attend your event personally, when you select this option, here you will have to provide the address of the place where you are going to organize the event as well as the date and time. You will also have to provide some details.

Step-6: After entering the details of the event, you have to tell whether your event ticket comes in different price or service, if yes then you have to select the variant option.

Under this, you will get many features so that you can create different types of event tickets.

If you want to add your guest at different places according to the facilities, then you can do it like for example you can make Variant like Platinum, Gold, Silver etc which will be different according to the price.

Step-7: After this you will get the option of edit in which you can set the price of your individual event at any time and here you will get the option to set different price for each variant.

Step-8: After this you get the option to select the category in which you have to select the category of the event.

Step-9: After this also you get the option of Reselling and SEO Optimize, about which we have already told you.

After selecting everything, your event ticket will be added to the online store and its link will be generated.

By creating an event link in this way, you can promote it on other platforms.

Nowadays people show a lot of activity towards the event, so it becomes easy to earn money by selling event tickets.

You can get paid for your event tickets through the payment link.

If you talk about other social media platforms, then you may not have all these features available there, which makes the task of selling tickets a bit difficult, but you have all the features available on Instamojo.

Also, here you can visit your online store from time to time to see what the response of the people you are getting.

7. By Selling Your Service

One way to earn money online is to earn money by selling your service.

On Instamojo, you can create links to your service and reach them to the customer.

Nowadays all the work has started being done online, so more and more people appear on such platforms where they get things according to their convenience.

Instamojo is also a popular platform, which is used by many people and today it is slowly becoming popular even among those who had never even heard of it.

Therefore, it is very easy to earn money by selling your service here and you can add any kind of service to your online store, by sharing the link in different platforms like Facebook, Instagram, WhatsApp etc., you can connect with the customer.

Here you can provide any kind of service like coaching, food, travel, freelance work, repairing work, online teaching and tutoring, translation and many more you can do under this.

For example, we can take freelancer work, today the demand for freelancer is very high and people are looking for such people on more and more online platforms who can do work like content writing, editing and translation for them.

If you have these skills, then you can prepare related posters and add them to your online store.

There will definitely be some people visiting your store who will need this kind of service and they will definitely contact you.

Apart from this, you can add to sell by writing content on many topics yourself and promote your service by creating a link to it.

When your service starts reaching people and they get the benefit of it, then your service becomes even more popular and on this platform you can also get paid for your service.

So in this way you can also earn money from Instamojo platform by selling your service.

8. Creating an Ecommerce Website

Creating an e-commerce website on most platforms and collecting payment by selling your products on it can be quite complicated, but on Instamojo, you can easily collect your payment by creating an e-commerce website.

There are many people who do not trust the manual process i.e. transferring money to the bank account but the simple features that are available on Instamojo prove to be quite trustworthy.

It is quite easy to earn money by creating an e-commerce website here, so let's know about it in detail-

As you know that nowadays the use of payment gateway has become very popular for e-commerce site and Instamojo is a popular payment gateway so let us know how to create Ecommerce website here and how to sell your products. You can receive payment.

To create an e-commerce website on Instamojo, you will first need to create your merchant account on Instamojo, for which you will need PAN card, bank account details and email ID.

You have already got the information about how to create an account on Instamojo.

When you have prepared your website by entering all the details, then you can earn money by uploading your product on the e-commerce website.

The biggest advantage of uploading a product on an e-commerce website is that any customer can buy your product through credit, debit or net banking and all the transactions that happen on your e-commerce website will be informed on that email id. You will get mail that you have registered.

Now the question comes that when you will get your payment, then let us tell you that your money in merchant account will be transferred to bank account within 3 days.

After creating a merchant account, you can control your Instamojo payment gateway as you wish, such as creating new product links, uploading products, or accessing APIs.

One thing to note is that initially your merchant account is like a trial account i.e. you can only do transactions up to Rs 10 thousand every month here but if you want to remove this limit then you can submit KYC which After this this limit of your e-commerce website will be removed and you will be able to do as many transactions as you want.

The e-commerce website provides you the facility that without any hassle, the transaction of money is done very easily and every customer also has the facility to make online payment, so by creating an e-commerce website, people can make their product or service. The way to reach is very good and a good amount of money can also be earned from it.

You get so many great features to create an e-commerce website in which more than 20 premium themes are available to you which gives your online business a professional look in front of the people.

Also on this website you can get the details of all the transactions from time to time by adding your domain and email.

Here you can also send SMS and email campaigns to your customers and run ads on your store, so creating an e-commerce website becomes a very good and easy way to earn money.

Various marketing tools are also available here which help in uploading and promoting your product easily.

You can also take out discount coupons on the e-commerce website, so that you can attract more and more customers towards you, with all these functions, the e-commerce website on Instamojo proves to be beneficial.

So if you want to upload your product on e-commerce website without using online store then you will not have any problem in this, you can fully trust this platform.

9. Becoming a Reseller

After so many options, you come across the way to earn money by becoming a reseller.

Reseller means selling someone's product and getting commission from them.

When we were telling you about adding a product on Instamojo, then we told you about an option in it called Reselling, using which you give your product to a person who helps in selling it. and receives some commission in return.

That's all you have to do.

If you want to earn money by becoming a reseller, then you can create an account on Instamojo and resell the products of those people who give you such options on their online store.

For example you can take Affiliate Marketing as you know that in Affiliate Marketing you promote the link of others product on your website and whenever someone buys the product through that link then you get its commission. .

Similar work is done by becoming a Reseller on Instamojo.

You can help sell people's product links on Instamojo by promoting them on various platforms and get commission from them.

Here whenever your customer buys this product, then you will get commission from the owner of that product.

The advantage of earning money by becoming a reseller is that you get a commission for selling every product and there are many people on Instamojo who want to enable the option of reselling and make their product reach as many people as possible, so you can easily Reselling work is available on this platform.

Here you can earn money in two ways, one way is that you can connect with more and more customers by sharing the link of the product on different platforms and the other is that you yourself help in selling the products of others through online store. Can do, both of these methods are very beneficial.

It is just like affiliate marketing, if you have a website, then you can earn money by promoting the link of the product on that too.

On doing affiliate marketing on Instamojo, you also get some commission from this platform for the new payment gateway user.

As you know, there is also an option of SEO setting in online store which is used to get your product ranked.

In such a situation, if you promote a link to a product from Instamojo on your website, then you can get even more benefits.

So money can also be earned by doing reselling work in this way.

If you compare Instamojo with the rest of the platform, then the work of affiliate marketing can be done there too, but there are not such features as are provided to you on Instamojo because by reselling here you can get your payment from this platform ie You can get commission from the product owner.

10. Invite and earn

Instamojo top 10 ways to earn money also include 'Invite and earn' which is also called Refer and earn, which means Invite and earn money.

There are many such platforms on social media which have not yet been able to reach all the people, that is, they are not popular everywhere and their users are not too many.

In such a situation, these platforms take out methods like Invite and Earn so that more and more people can reach their service and use it so that they can earn more and more money.

One such platform is Instamojo in which this option is available.

Although it is a very popular payment gateway of India, but most of the people still use the foreign platform, so you will see the option of Invite and Earn on Instamojo, through which you will reach it to the people, in return you will get commission through this platform.

Using this, you can earn money from your mobile anytime and anywhere while sitting at home or even outside the house.

On Instamojo platform you get the opportunity that you can earn money just by sharing its link.

After creating your profile on Instamojo, when you will see on your dashboard, you will see an option of Invite and Earn on the left corner on which you have to click.

Here you are given a referral code along with the referral link which you have to share with your friends, relatives or others.

You can use social media platforms like Facebook, Instagram and WhatsApp etc. to share.

500 bonus cash is given to you by the Instamojo platform whenever a person creates his profile on Instamojo through the link shared by you.

On Instamojo, you are given different commissions for different work, let us understand about you in a little detail-

You can see that you get a premium subscription on Instamojo by visiting their online store.

Instamojo will give you one thousand rupees commission if any person buys growth annual subscription of premium online store of instamojo through the code referred by you.

Similarly, if a person creates his profile on Instamojo and makes his first transaction through your referral link, then you are given Rs 500 as commission.

That is, if you have shared the referral code and referral link, if he buys a product or course on Instamojo, then you get money.

Are you wondering why someone would use Instamojo through the link you refer?

Because he can also login directly by downloading the Instamojo app.

So let us tell you that not only you benefit here, but the one who has created the profile through the referral link also benefits.

Whoever creates an account on Instamojo through a referral link and buys a premium plan called Annual Growth Subscription on the online store, he gets a discount of one thousand rupees and the second benefit is that after doing the first transaction He gets 5000 Mojo Plus Points and using these points one can pay transaction fees and shipping.

Also, these points can be used in other business apps as well.

In this way, you can also create money by inviting people.

Looking at the benefits given here, every person will definitely think about using it once, so if you share it among more and more people, then your chances of getting maximum benefit increase.

The more people who join the Instamojo platform using the link and code you refer, the more commission you will get.

If you want, you can also take some advantage yourself by using the refer link and code provided by someone else.

Conclusion

These were the easiest ways to earn money through instamojo payment gateway, using which you can easily earn money sitting at home.

You will see so many great functions here that your every task will become easy and you will not need any other social media app.

In this way you know what a great platform Instamojo is where many things can be done.

You have seen how many options there are on this popular platform to earn money and you have got all the information about it.

All these methods are very easy and you can easily do all the work sitting at home.

All the options given to you here are very popular in the market and people like them are very much attracted, so your chances of earning money increase a lot.

On Instamojo, you get all the features that you need because every little thing has been taken care of on this platform, so that business people do not have any problem.

The features that you get on foreign online payment platforms, you get them here too and because it is India's own online payment platform.

Therefore, it is also very trustworthy, online shopping is very much in trend today and more and more people do online shopping.

Along with this, people's work has also been made very easy in online payment, so instead of cash, people have started relying on online payment only.

You can say that it is much better than other payment gateways because all kinds of online product sales and payments take place here.

Many people use this platform, but they may not have complete knowledge about them, so if you are also one of those people, then we hope that here you have got all the information you need and you will get some new information. You must have also come to know about the option so that you can earn extra money by doing some work on them too.

The purpose of writing this article was to let you know about some new features and features that will make your work easier.

Hope you liked this article and will provide you new options to earn money through this platform.

If you want to know about some such new ways by which you can create extra money, then stay connected with us, we will keep telling you new ways to earn money online for you.

53

Please write a review about this book.